MW01167333

Stressbusting

For the 21st Century

Access Limitless Immune System-Boosting
Endorphins that Wipe Out Stress and Promote
Good Health

The Stressbusting Workshop

For info about upcoming U.K. seminars and events, contact:

stress.b.events@gmail.com

Table of Contents

Introduction

Why stressbusting should be everyone's number one priority

In the 21st century, stress is linked to the six leading causes of death. In these technology-driven times, we're subjected to a blitz of information and expectations that make the cognitive load we juggle greater than ever. Cortisol, the hormone our bodies manufacture when stressed, manifests as anxiety, depression, overthinking, irritability, high blood pressure, OCD, rapid weight gain, premature ageing, asthma, diabetes and Alzheimer's. Cortisol also suppresses and weakens our immune system, making us more susceptible to respiratory infections and illnesses like cancer.

In contrast, our bodies are powerhouses at creating endorphins (dopamine, serotonin, and oxytocin) that counteract stress, boost our immune system, and improve health and well-being. It may not feel like it, but our bodies are as enthusiastic about providing us with these much-needed endorphins as they clearly are about making cortisol. Sadly, due to the relentless nature of modern living, we've lost touch with the natural prompts to make this happen regularly. Stressbusting For the 21st Century will equip you with proven techniques that flip the coin from negative to positive and let your body know, safely and naturally, that it's okay to focus on making stressbusting, health-promoting endorphins from now on. The positive effect this will have on your mental and physical well-being in the short, medium and long term is immeasurable.

One

The Green and Red Powerhouse Factories

It's as though we have two factories, side by side, in our chest. A Green Factory that makes endorphins that boost our immune system, and a Red Factory that manufactures the stress hormone Cortisol. The Green Factory is connected to our pleasure centre and goes to work whenever we're experiencing something uplifting, thrilling or heart-warming. By contrast, The Red Factory is connected to our fight-or-flight response. It goes to work whenever our primitive survival response places an order and furiously manufactures cortisol that makes us either want to take flight from a perceived threat (stressed/anxious) or curl up into a ball of dread and hide away from it (depressed). As discussed, the cortisol required for this affects our health negatively and weakens our immune system.

Down at the factories

So, what dictates whether it's your Red Factory's turn to manufacture stress-causing cortisol or your Green Factory's to make immune system-boosting endorphins? Reassuringly, the answer to this question is you.

The Rollercoaster Ride

Some people love rollercoasters and receive an endorphin high when riding them, while for others, they represent a stress-inducing nightmare. But what dictates why some people love the feeling of that first uncontrollable plunge while others would rather be anywhere else on earth? The answer lies in their reaction to the ride. For those who consider rollercoasters a positive experience, their response to the rollercoaster's ups and downs, twists and turns communicates to their factories that, far from facing a threat that requires their Red Factory to produce cortisol, it's the turn of their Green Factory to put the pedal to the metal, treating them to endorphins that make them want to seek the positive experience out again. Thanks to the excellent work of their Green Factory, when they climb out of their seat at the end of the ride, their eyes are crystal clear and twinkling, their complexion is glowing, and their energy levels are through the roof, all due to endorphins having given their immune system a massive boost. Contrast this to the person who found the ride a nerve-wracking experience. As a result of the work of their Red Factory, when they climb off the ride, they're pale and shaky, their eyes are rheumy with fear, and they are drained and listless, all because of the cortisol that pummelled their immune system. Modern life's ups and downs are akin to a rollercoaster ride. And like the rollercoaster ride, how we respond to it dictates whether our Green or Red Factories spring into action for us.

Two

The physical request for endorphins
or
The F.D.A Method

In the second half of this book, we will provide you with a powerful, cutting-edge **mental** technique that instructs your Green Factory to get to work on your behalf. Along with proven ways to stop stressful thoughts and prevent overthinking. But we will start with the F.D.A. Method. The F.D.A. Method is a skill set that, once mastered, will enable you to **physically** instruct your Green Factory to manufacture endorphins that neutralise stress and boost your immune system on demand.

If you've been stressed, run-down or prone to anxiety, depression, or overthinking, it's because, through no fault of your own, you've been calling for assistance from your Red Factory. It seems unkind, but Mother Nature has provided us with a direct, easily triggered line to our Red Factory. It's our default position, lest a now non-existent lion should be waiting to pounce around the next corner. And due to the demanding and nonstop nature of our modern lives, it's as though the threat of wild animals lurks everywhere (are attached to every issue).

Rest assured that, from this day forward, the F.D.A. Method will provide you with a direct means of communication with your Green Factory, empowering you to inform it that lions are no longer attached to a particular issue or your life in general. That 'I'm embracing the ride, so get to work and manufacture endorphins for me!`

This life-changing message is sent to your Green Factory by emphatically utilising muscles in three areas. The most obvious but by no means the most important are the muscles in your face, which contort to form a smile when you're happy. This gently communicates that you're not threatened by the thoughts that have arrived on your conscious 'screen` or what you're encountering in the outside world. But the face muscles are minuscule compared to the second Green Factory message muscle, one of the biggest and most flexible in the human body: the diaphragm.

Your diaphragm is inside your rib cage, resembling a giant elastic band stretching horizontally from one side of your rib cage to the other. Whenever you breathe in, your diaphragm moves down and assists in sucking air into your lungs as it does so. The longer you inhale, the further your diaphragm travels down towards your waist and the more uncomfortable you feel. This is because our diaphragm is pulled down and stretched into its most taut position when we breathe in. When we breathe out again, much of the relief we experience is due to the diaphragm moving back up and relaxing again.

The third and final set of Green Factory message muscles are the abdominal muscles. The abdominal muscles are as important as the diaphragm in sending a message that you're embracing the ride and to manufacture endorphins for you. Let's locate your abs now. Bring a thumb and middle finger on the same hand together so they touch, then draw them apart to create a prong. Place this prong (your thumb and middle finger) against your abs (horizontally) on either side of and just above your belly button. Now, exhale **forcibly** and feel how your abs move **inwards** as you do.

An important realisation

Whenever we are involved in an enjoyable, uplifting activity, the emphasis of our breathing is always on the exhalation – when we laugh, cheer, sing, whistle a tune, or groan because we're enjoying a good massage. During all these activities (and **any other** pleasurable activity you can think of), the emphasis of our breathing is always on the exhalation, never on the inhalation. Let's take this analogy to its ultimate conclusion.

Back on the rollercoaster

What dictates why some people love the feeling of that first uncontrollable plunge while others would rather be anywhere else on earth? The answer is their reaction to it. For those who consider the rollercoaster a positive experience, their response as it begins its first big plunge is to smile, hold up a clenched fist and exhale with a cry of "ALL RIGHT!" A response that causes their **diaphragm to move up and relax and their abs to move inwards and tighten as they assist in forcing the air from their lungs**. This communicates to their factories that, far from facing a threat that requires their Red Factory to make Cortisol, their Green Factory treats them to a massive release of endorphins. Conversely, the person sitting next to them who responded to the same plunge by taking a deep breath that **lowers and tightens their diaphragm and expands their abs** while adopting a stricken expression is subjected to a massive release of Cortisol. A panic attack is the worst-case scenario should the Red Factory go all out.

Calling the Green Factory!

A sudden exhalation with the **specific muscular activity involved** is the primary way we communicate to the Green Factory that, far from being threatened by an idea or situation, we're embracing it, so get to work on those endorphins.

The folly of responding to anything by taking a breath

When we respond to our thoughts or things occurring in the outside world with an intake of breath, it communicates that we are wary of it. For instance, when we hear bad news, a reminder of a problem arrives on our conscious screen, or when we stumble and must prevent a fall. Indeed, the moment we hear/think/experience anything unpleasant, we react by drawing a breath, and this 'under threat` message is relayed to our Red Factory. It is, therefore, counterproductive to respond to **anything** in this way. In the 21st century, even on those rare occasions when you might find yourself in a genuine emergency, like having to evacuate a building due to fire, it's far better to remain calm and have your wits about you than be in a cortisol-induced panic.

Three

F.D.A Method Training First Steps

You are now aware of what you need to do in response to thoughts that arrive on your conscious screen or occurrences in the outside world that would typically trigger stress or anxiety: utilise your diaphragm and abs to send a message to your Green Factory that says, "Far from being threatened, I'm embracing this!" Once mastered, you will move out of the roller-coaster (of life's) Red Factory seat and into one where your Green Factory is batting for you.

The balloon method

We have trialled many versions but found the Balloon Method ticks all the boxes to ensure that the F.D.A. Muscles do *precisely* what they need to do to send this all-important message to the Green Factory.

Warning

You may feel light-headed while practising the following exercises. If so, take a break whenever necessary.

Let's start by blowing up some imaginary balloons

Place the tips of your thumb and middle finger (of the same hand) on either side and just above your belly button and apply a little pressure to feel and be **certain that your abdominal muscles are moving in** as you blow up each imaginary balloon. The exhalation you're about to produce should be strong and measured (just as it would need to be if you were blowing up a real balloon), and it should last approximately five seconds. To avoid getting too light-headed, it is advised that you wait for at least thirty seconds in between blowing up your imaginary balloons.

Please blow up three imaginary balloons in the way described above.

During the exercise, you should have felt and ensured your abdominal muscles **moved inwards** as you blew air into your imaginary balloons. Of course, during your exhalation, your diaphragm would have automatically moved up into its most relaxed position. As your diaphragm does what it needs to do automatically during your exhalation, please don't worry about that important muscle from now on. Your attention should be focused on ensuring that your abdominal muscles move **inwards and tighten** while blowing up each balloon.

Four

The Green Factory Operational Zone

When you enter the Green Factory Operational
Zone, your abs, diaphragm, and face muscles
will be in their happiest position as far as your
Green Factory is concerned. Why the happiest?
Think about when a friend has said something so
funny that you've doubled over with laughter.
At these times, your abdominal muscles will
have tightened to the point where **all the air** has
been expelled from your lungs, and you can't
breathe. At such times, with tears streaming
down your face, you may start gesticulating to
your friend to stop making you laugh because
you need to steal a breath. You need to steal a
breath because your mirth expelled the air from
your lungs. Apart from a coughing fit, your
abdominal muscles only ever contract in this
severe way during these happiest moments. This
results in your being treated to immune-boosting

endorphins to match the experience. The Green Factory Operational Zone is designed to allow you to surreptitiously **mimic** those occasions when you're laughing so hysterically that you can barely breathe for several seconds. During life's daily rollercoaster ride, when you do this in response to pangs of anxiety or dread or the arrival of troubling thoughts that would typically see you reacting in a way that asks your Red Factory for assistance, it **instead** communicates to your Green Factory that far from being threatened by this situation or issue, you now consider them the funniest, least threatening things to stumble sideways across the earth. If you repeatedly respond to the arrival of specific thoughts or pangs of anxiety or dread in this way, you **re-train** your mind that all is well with this issue, so reminding and stressing you out about it is no longer required. As far as you're concerned, all may not be well with this issue. But the assistance of your Red Factory to 'help` you with it is the very last thing you need. Again, like exiting a burning building, dealing with any of life's issues is best done in a calm and determined frame of mind—one with the added benefit of not damaging your health.

Five

Training Part 1:
Entering the Green Factory Operational Zone

1. Make a prong from your thumb and middle finger and place this prong on either side of and just above your belly button. As you did earlier, apply some pressure so you can feel and be sure that your abdominal muscles move in and tighten as you exhale.

2. You're about to blow up an imaginary balloon. So, produce a strong and sustained exhalation **(from your abs!)** just as you would need to if you were blowing up a real balloon: keep blowing in a **single long exhale** until you've expelled all the air from your lungs and your abs feel as tight as they would if you were laughing hysterically and then, holding your tightened abs in place by **not breathing air back**

into your stomach, smile and breathe shallowly from your upper chest.

If you have followed the above directions correctly, you will have expelled as much air from your belly as you can using your abs, and you'll be holding your tightened abs in place by breathing into your upper chest and not your stomach.

How long should you remain in the Green Factory Operational Zone and breathe shallowly from your upper chest in this way? In the initial learning stages, you should stay in the Zone, your abs tightened to their fullest by exhalation, and breathing into your upper chest for approximately 10 seconds. The amount of time you can spend in this Zone will increase the more proficient you become at entering it. Please practise entering the Green Factory Operational Zone a few times before moving on. When you leave the Zone, your initial breath **can** be deep and relieving.

Exiting the Green Factory Operational Zone

While inside the Zone, you will have been
denying your body oxygen precisely as you do
whenever you laugh hysterically. For this reason,
when you leave it by taking a normal breath
(relaxing your abs) and breathing from your
belly again, you'll discover that this initial breath
is naturally deep, enjoyable, and brings a sense
of relief. This is one of those few occasions when
taking a deep breath feels and is beneficial. Why?
Because it provides the same sensation of relief
as when, for instance, you have swum the length
of a pool underwater, burst through the surface,
and taken that first gulp of wonderful air. This
need to take a big, refreshing gulp of air adds a
sense of euphoria to the excellent work you've
just done, creating endorphins in the Green
Factory Operational Zone. This need to take a
deep breath when you exit the Zone indicates
that you entered it successfully. In fact, the
bigger the breath **you naturally need** to take
when you leave the Zone, shows how well you
entered it. If you exit the Zone and do not need
to take a deep, relieving breath, it indicates that

you baulked or didn't apply the no-nonsense
effort required when you entered the Zone. More
on that shortly.

Six

The Immune System Boosting Endorphin Sponge

While in the Green Factory Operational Zone, the corners of your mouth will be raised into a smile, and you'll be breathing shallowly from your upper chest. To ensure that your abs remain as **tight as possible**, **use them** (your abs) to puff and send **quick bursts** of air out of your mouth that will further tighten your abs. Doing this will provide you with, for want of a better term, a valve that you can use to squeeze the maximum number of endorphins from your abdominal or endorphin sponge.

This tightening and holding of your abs (as though in mid-hysterical laugh) is vital to producing endorphins. It can, therefore, be helpful to imagine that a sponge is between your abdominal muscles and the more you **tighten**

your abs by exhaling from them, the greater the number of endorphins you squeeze from the sponge. Again, you're mimicking what your abs, diaphragm (and face if you're smiling) are doing whenever you find something hysterically funny. With practice, you will discover that when squeezed to the maximum, this sponge has a sweet spot that takes the release of endorphins to the next level. What is required from you to hit the sponge's sweet spot? Effort – maximum effort in blowing up your imaginary balloon and tightening your abs **just that little bit further** than you imagined possible.

Practice makes perfect, and once you're adept at entering the Green Factory Operational Zone and remaining there for 10+ seconds, the world is your oyster as far as the creation of immune system-boosting endorphins is concerned.

Seven

Time to take stock of how you feel

Once the euphoria of taking that big, relieving inhalation has passed when you exit the Green Factory Operational Zone, it's time to take stock of how you feel. Suppose you were feeling anxious or depressed when you entered the Zone. In that case, it depends entirely upon the amount of fight or flight chemicals (cortisol) that were present in your system as to how long it takes to flush them out of it and replace them with the endorphins you're creating. It may be that more endorphin troops are needed on the battlefield. Remember, you have a **limitless supply** at your disposal. So, re-enter the Green Factory Operational Zone, squeeze that sponge for all you're worth, and once again command your Green Factory to provide endorphins. Your mind/body system is programmed is to manufacture endorphins <u>whenever</u> your abdominal, diaphragm and facial muscles react in this decisive and unequivocal way.

Mimicking mirth
When entering the Green Factory Operational Zone (if alone), it can be beneficial to do so with an exhalation where you hiss *'Heeeeeeee!'* under your breath.

A quick demonstration
Place the prong of your thumb and forefinger on either side of your belly button. Now impersonate a laugh by hissing *'he, he, he, he, he,'* and feel how markedly your abdominal muscles move in towards the sweet spot of the sponge.

You may discover that blowing up your balloon with a hissed, five-second *'Heeeeeeeee!'* is more effective for tightening your abs to their maximum than simply blowing up the balloon in the usual way. Again, when alone, some people also find that producing a low growl while blowing up the balloon can be empowering.

Others like to squeeze a sports hand grip (used for strengthening hands) to the closed position as they exhale and blow up their imaginary balloon. Experiment and go with what feels the most effective for you. The most important thing is that you grow adept at contracting your abdominal muscles by **exhaling from them**, holding them tightly in place, and then using the air you're breathing into your chest to exhale and tighten them more, if necessary, with short, sharp bursts (page 24). The greater the ratcheting of your abdominal muscles (which mimics what they do when you're laughing hysterically or being thrilled by a roller-coaster ride), the greater the production of endorphins for the battlefield to replace cortisol. Once in the Green Factory Operational Zone, the air you breathe into your **upper chest** is the **perfect ammunition** for this exhaling/ratcheting of the abs process.

Greater physical strength

You will also discover that you will be provided with significantly more strength when you exhale from your abs (and hold them) before lifting something. This extra strength is a testament to the excellent place your mind/body system enters whenever you utilise your abdominal muscles in this positive way. Exhaling in this manner during exercise will produce massive amounts of immune system-boosting endorphins.

Eight

Green Factory Zone Training Part 2: The Golf-Ball-Sized Balloon

While out-and-out determination is required to blow up a full-size imaginary balloon when addressing significant anxiety or dread and entering the Green Factory Operational Zone, a less heavy-duty response will be sufficient when encountering smaller twangs of stress/anxiety/dread regarding minor issues or situations. These twangs are akin to a single butterfly of anxiety entering your belly. In the past, you would have reacted to this butterfly by **taking** a breath, which drew more butterflies in to join the first. This amounts to instructing your Red Factory to manufacture cortisol for you. So, the best course of action is to **expel any initial butterflies** using your abs and then enter a less intense version of the Green Factory Operational Zone to prevent them from returning. This will also instruct your Green Factory to manufacture endorphins instead, albeit more leisurely, as it better suits the more relaxed nature of the positive experience you're apparently having. This is most effectively achieved by replacing the full-sized imaginary balloon with a golf-ball-sized balloon.

A balloon the size of a golf ball would require only a single, sharp puff of air to inflate – a short, sharp burst from your abs that instantly expels the butterfly. So, let's try that now. Place your prong on either side of your belly button (to ensure the inward movement of your abs when you exhale) and blow up a golf ball-sized balloon with a **single and decisive** exhalation/puff that lasts half a second. Now, hold your **slightly** tightened abs in place and breathe in and out through your nose into your chest. This ensures that the butterfly (of anxiety or dread) you have just expelled from your belly cannot return there. That single butterfly in your stomach indicated that an issue in your mind has just prodded you gently and enquired, "I don't suppose *this* information is still a threat?" A quick exhale and entering the golf-ball-sized zone will reply: 'No, it isn't. So, I do not need to overthink it **or** the assistance of my Red Factory/fight or flight response to deal with it.`

This mini version of entering the Green Factory Operational Zone is a great place to be in general. We recommend going there whenever you are experiencing a stressful time or even when you aren't. Since it's entered using a quick exhalation that produces only a slight tightening of the abs, it's not in the least bit uncomfortable, and yet produces low levels of endorphins that help to keep you calm and focused.

Remember, while in this mini version of the Green Factory Operational Zone, it's important that you hold your slightly tightened abs in place, breathe in and out from your chest, and raise the corners of your mouth into a self-assured smile that suits the more considered nature of this mini-Zone. Due to its relaxed nature, you can remain in it for as long as you like. As well as keeping cortisol at bay (by keeping the fight/flight response in check), the low levels of endorphins you're creating will boost your immune system and assist in keeping you healthy. You also look thinner due to an **exhale** keeping your abs held in. The opposite of sucking in your stomach that's as harmful (Red Factory signalling) as it sounds.

Nine

Guaranteed panic attack prevention

For your body to trigger and sustain a panic attack, **you must supply it with considerable extra oxygen**. If you refuse, it cannot go into panic attack mode. If this sounds comforting, it ought to be. It means that the power is in your hands to prevent panic attacks. The air we breathe is required to sustain our bodily functions. The mind/body system can't afford to divert oxygen away from our vital organs to engage in the luxury of a panic attack. This is why it requires us to breathe deeply and supply it with this extra oxygen (hyperventilate). Just as a car's engine cannot run without petrol, a panic attack cannot run without you anxiously sucking air into your lungs to make it happen. For this reason, responding to the onset of a panic attack with a powerful exhale and entering the Green

Factory Operational Zone will stop a panic attack in its tracks every time.

Ten

Beware of baulking!

This brings us to the only thing that now stands between you and a life free of being subjected to your fight or flight response/Red Factory constantly overreacting on your behalf. Balking. If a racehorse approaches a difficult fence that it doesn't think it can get over, it will come to an abrupt halt, sometimes throwing its rider to the ground. The horse has baulked at the idea of jumping the fence. If you abandon your plan to enter the Green Factory Operational Zone and continue as before, it will be because of the myriad of doubts that flew into your mind and told you to give up and throw in the towel – that resisting is futile. The old and predictable favourites: "Are you *crazy*? What are you *doing*? This is NEVER going to work! It's much too difficult! You haven't got the energy or time for this nonsense!" etc.

The best way of dealing with negativity is to turn it into positivity by using its weight against it. This is achieved by looking upon pangs of anxiety or dread not as things to recoil from as in the past but as **prompts and reminders** to enter either the full-on Green Factory Operational Zone and **squeeze that endorphin sponge** for all you're worth or else to utilise the mini zone and produce lower levels of endorphins over a more extended period. If you adjust your mindset to respond to stress/spiralling feelings this way and instead make them your **triggers to do something positive**, nothing can stand in your way. The good news is that responding to anxiety or stressful thoughts this way is far easier than you might imagine. It's simply a case of **awareness** and then moving into the **positive response seat** on the rollercoaster.

Eleven

Practise your new skills!

Practice makes perfect, and practising going into
the Green Factory Operational Zone will stand
you in good stead for when you find yourself in
a genuinely stressful situation. Ideally, once
you've mastered your two new responses (full-
sized balloon response and golf-ball-sized
balloon response), you will have someone who
can assist you in practising them. This is best
achieved by asking your helper to stand behind
you. After some time (from a few seconds to a
minute), they should grab your shoulder and
attempt to startle you. This grab/startle
represents the moment an anxiety-inducing
question is posed to your conscious screen, or
you feel a butterfly of anxiety in your belly.
When they grab your shoulder, it's your cue to
exhale from your abs, blow up your balloon,
smile, and shallow-breathe into your chest.

Learning from initial confusion

The first few times you attempt to enter the Green Factory Operational Zone when under attack from anxiety or dread, the balking thoughts may convince you to stop or put in a half-hearted effort. If this happens, don't get disheartened. It's an opportunity to learn. Think about what you did during those vital few seconds when you were *supposed* to enter the Zone convincingly but didn't. Think about the doubts your mind used to deter you and **be alert** and ready for them the next time. You will soon learn to stick to your guns, enter the Zone, and squeeze the life out of the sponge regardless. The alternative? Passively allowing the fight or flight response/your Red Factory to bring you to your knees by stressing you out/making you anxious or depressed by producing cortisol. No longer acceptable now you can communicate directly with your Green Factory and instruct it to take over.

Zero Tolerance Towards overthinking, anxiety, or dread

Going forward, make zero tolerance your policy towards any feeling of anxiety or dread. Respond to butterflies or twinges of dread with your balloon response. Once again: your mind/body system has an unlimited supply of immune system boosting endorphins to put at your disposal. So why allow any feelings of anxiety or dread to go unchecked? Squeeze your abdominal sponge and instruct your Green Factory to make endorphins to counteract and replace the cortisol. When ambushed by anxious thoughts/pangs of anxiety, you have a choice: fight back with the weapons you now have at your disposal or passively submit to them. A component of the fight or flight response is designed to render you passive. To make you feel hopeless. **This feeling is an illusion**. You can always fight back. You must fight back. **And this means instructing your Green Factory to take over from the Red Factory and get to work.** The quality of your life depends upon your doing so – embrace the rollercoaster of life. Send your Green Factory the message: "The threats are miles behind me now! I'm embracing life's ride and what's before me!"

Part one of this book focused on the physical tools you need to neutralise stress and instruct your Green Factory to manufacture immune system boosting endorphins. We recommend mastering these tools before moving on to part 2 which will provide mental tools to achieve the same thing. Each can be used individually. And when combined, they provide the nuclear option for neutralising stress and creating endorphins.

Stressbusting
For the 21st Century

Part Two

**The mental instruction to your Green
Factory to create endorphins**

Twelve

Laying the mental groundwork. Why are we so prone to overthinking and stress?

The human mind is packed with individual memory cells. We call them oases because they resemble tiny pools of electrical energy that store information. Most of your oases are friendly and valuable. For instance, if you own a dog, it will be the job of your Dog Oasis to store and safeguard the information/your memories about your dog. This oasis is tasked with delivering the information about your dog to your conscious 'screen` when you 'cast` for it or when it's needed. For instance, your Dog Oasis is responsible for reminding you that it's time to feed your dog. If you forget, it will be because **another, stronger oasis** in your mind has sent what it considers to be more pressing information to your conscious screen and got you overthinking the information inside its file.

As a result, your Dog Oasis is shut out from your screen and must wait its turn before bursting back and reminding you (in your own voice in your mind), 'You haven't fed Fido!`

These individual oases with their own agendas battle for our attention throughout the day (and night in the form of dreams), which explains why we always have something on our minds. They like nothing better than for us to mull over the information inside their file. Why? Because the more time we spend overthinking (or stressing over) the information about a specific person, place, thing, or problem inside the file of an oasis, the more electrical energy it's gifted, and the stronger and higher up the hierarchy of our oases it climbs. What's more, for a dominant oasis to remain so, it must bully its way back onto your screen and coax you into thinking about the information inside its file as often as it can.

Don't take the bait, Charlie!

Oases aim to get us back inside their files by asking us questions crafted to tempt us back. For example, if Charlie is worried about a mole following a recent visit to the doctor, a question Charlie's recently formed Mole Oasis might ask to get Charlie stressing over any and everything connected to the mole and the visit to the doctor might be. "It was good of the doctor to see you quickly and be reassuring. But the expression on his face when he said goodbye was anything but reassuring. What's he not telling you and why!?" Unaware that this question is simply the bait that the Mole Oasis has used to draw Charlie back into its file, Charlie dives in and overthinks the encounter with the doctor again—not achieving anything remotely helpful and becoming increasingly stressed while in there. And, what's more, while Charlie's inside this file dwelling on the visit again, the Mole Oasis is enjoying a buffet of electrical energy, which means it will be strong enough to return to Charlie's screen with a similar question to get Charlie overthinking the encounter with the doctor when next it fancies a bite. This is the very epitome of a stressful overthinking circle that needs to be broken.

Thirteen

YOU are the captain of your thoughts

Although your oases are a part of you, they are also separate from you. In this respect, you are the captain on the flight deck with a view of where you're going and access to the controls. Your oases are your rowdy crew, jostling at the door, trying to catch your attention and intent on getting you to think about the information inside their files and even influence you.

<u>Vigilance is the best place to start</u>

Paying attention to and developing an awareness of the questions and tactics your oases use to tempt you back inside their files will increase your understanding of how your mind works and enable you to become a stricter, far less stressed captain. The more observant you are, the less your oases will have free reign to run roughshod and coax you back into their files to re-tread the same old ground in search of answers.

Not so fun but useful fact

The answers to problems are rarely located in these files. They contain only the same questions that lead to being tempted back into these files to re-tread old ground, triggering stress, anxiety, or depression.

Wakey, wakey, rise and shine

An excellent opportunity to study and gauge the hierarchy of your oases and their tactics occurs first thing in the morning when you wake up. That's when, having formed an orderly queue that's dictated by their strength (itself dictated by how much time you've spent in their files of late), they are chomping at the bit to burst onto your screen and present their information, i.e., "Consider this topic/information/potential problem." Taking this bait is akin to giving these

oases an all-they-can-eat buffet of electrical
energy for breakfast.

The good news about the genuine answers to the problems we seek

The answers we need tend to come when
relaxing, switching off, listening to music,
enjoying a movie, or similar entertainment.
That's when helpful oases can take advantage of
the calm to make it to our screens and deliver the
information or solution we've requested or cast
for earlier. These helpful oases will take care of
themselves, so let's get back to the troublesome,
stress-inducing ones needing a stricter captain.

Bait in the form of images

The questions that draw us back into files to
stress over problems can also be delivered to our
conscious screen as images. For instance, in the
case of Charlie's Mole, the Mole Oasis would
typically place an image of the less-than-
reassuring look on the doctor's face on Charlie's
screen. Doubtless, one of the first things Charlie

sees in his mind's eye when waking up the following day. Unaware that this image has been presented by a hungry oasis as bait, it will be enough to lure Charlie back into the file to overthink the encounter with his doctor.

Earworm tunes

So, to reiterate, while your oases are a part of you, they are also separate from you. This truth is never more evident than when topics you'd rather not think about keep returning to your screen and refuse to leave you alone. A helpful analogy would be when you can hear a song playing in your mind, having just heard it. It may be a song you loathe, but no matter how much you try to get rid of it, it outstays its welcome and continues to play. You would never think about a song you can't stand by choice. In case you were wondering why the infernal song clings on for dear life, it's because the oasis of this particular song enjoys the feed of electrical activity it receives while you're inside its file, reliving the memory of the song, just like all your other oases do.

Fourteen

How our oases play a significant role in our decision-making

The following Lost in the Desert Analogy demonstrates how oases also influence our decision-making.

Charlie is lost in the desert. Charlie is desperately tired but also thirsty, so he has two opposing oases in his mind: his Rest Oasis and Thirst Oasis. Charlie's Rest Oasis, responsible for ensuring he doesn't die of exhaustion, will tell him, 'Stop here and rest! You're exhausted!`

Meanwhile, Charlie's Thirst Oasis, tasked with ensuring he doesn't die of thirst, will be muscling in on his screen and saying, 'No. You can't rest yet. You must keep walking and find water. Otherwise, you'll die of thirst!` These opposing oases will battle for supremacy in Charlie's mind and attempt to persuade him to follow their instructions to either rest or to struggle on and find water. One of these oases has access to an emergency lever to get its way whether Charlie likes it or not. Can you guess which one it is? The answer will follow the next paragraph.

The longer we allow two opposing oases free rein to put their opposing arguments to us, the longer it takes us to make a decision and the more drained we feel.

The answer is Charlie's Sleep Oasis, which can make him pass out.

Fifteen

The real culprits of stress, anxiety, or depression:
Trip-Wire Oases

Much like the Sleep Oasis can make us pass out, a Trip-Wire Oases can make us stressed or anxious by alerting our Red Factory. The following example demonstrates how this occurs.

<u>Free-fall</u>

You're distracted by something pleasant and feeling okay when, from nowhere, you experience a pang of anxiety in the form of a sudden butterfly in your stomach or a sinking feeling as a dark cloud descends. A voice in the back of your mind (a trip-wire oasis) accompanies this unwelcome sensation and **basically** asks in your own voice or with an image plastered across your screen: 'Are the things associated with **THIS** a threat to you?`

Your unease intensifies, so you take a deeper breath to compensate, sucking more butterflies into your stomach, and your face adopts an anxious expression which tells the Trip-Wire Oases, "Apparently so!"

The Trip-Wire Oasis probes you again and **basically** asks: "Is there ANY CHANCE that the things associated with this question or image aren't a threat?"

Your growing unease sends the clear reply: "There's no chance whatsoever!"

And so, to "protect" you from this threat, the Trip-Wire Oasis triggers your Red Factory/fight or flight response and floods your system with cortisol. The FDA Method in part one of this book is a physical means of preventing free-fall.

The **mental skills** to counteract and override free-fall and direct your Green Factory to create

endorphins instead are made possible from
within The Mind Theatre.

Sixteen

The Mind Theatre

Only an unequivocal positive mental message will send trip-wire oases on their way, flip the coin from negative to positive, and instruct your Green Factory to manufacture endorphins instead of triggering free-fall. To send this new mental message, we need to make your mind more tangible. Getting a clear perspective on your mind is tricky because your mind is you, and you are it. It isn't easy to see the woods for the trees because you are the woods and the trees. So, let's do something about that and give you a heightened view of yourself with The Mind Theatre.

When you reach the end of this paragraph, we'd like you to look up from your book or device and drink in the view for several seconds. Please do that now.

Even though you have two eyes, you obviously didn't see two separate images. If you did book an appointment to visit two ophthalmologists. What you see is akin to an **all-encompassing Imax screen pressed against your face, showing your life occurring in real time.**

Let's switch the lights on inside your Mind or **Mind Theatre** and separate the woods from the trees.

We'd like you to imagine a circular room about the size of a living room. In the centre of this room or personal theatre is a swivel chair facing a floor-to-ceiling screen that wraps around its front half. This extraordinary screen takes up **all** your peripheral vision, left and right and up and down, **just like your view of the world does through your eyes.** Behind your swivel chair, and therefore behind you, another screen is wrapped around the back half of the circular theatre. On this screen is a mirror image of whatever you're observing on your front screen in the outside world. So, for instance, if you were looking at the view from your bedroom window (as displayed on your front screen), a mirror image of that view would be displayed on the screen behind you.

Finally, rising before your swivel chair, within easy reach, is a Lever. A Lever that can be locked to the left or right side, like those used to switch train tracks from left to right and back again.

The Lever is locked on the right side

Whenever you're focused on or paying attention to what's happening in the outside world (on your front screen), your Lever is pulled to the right side, two o'clock position. This is because observing or focusing on something outside involves using the right side of your mind. So, for instance, when successfully paying attention to a favourite drama on TV, your Lever will be in the right-side position as you view it through your screen.

The Lever is locked on the left side

If, during the drama, you are distracted by your thoughts, it's because an oasis has successfully pulled the Lever into the left side 10 o'clock position and brought your attention with it into its file. When this occurs, even though it appears to others that you're still watching the show, you aren't because your focus has switched to your thoughts – as though your chair has swivelled 180 degrees to face the back of your theatre, where the file of an oasis has replaced the screen's mirror image. While viewing these memories or concerns **inwardly**, you will miss what's happening in the show.

A crucial realisation

Your focus (and your Lever) can only be locked in **one** of these two positions at any moment. It's either locked in the right-side position, which means your focus is on the outside world through your screen and you're **living in the moment**, or in the left-side position, which means your focus has switched to being **inward** on your thoughts in a file. This awareness of how your focus and your Lever can only be in **one** of these two positions at any given moment (and never in between) is hugely important in instructing your Green Factory to create endorphins.

The battle for your attention

Throughout the day, a constant tug-of-war takes place in your mind. It's between your desire to focus on what you're doing or enjoying through your screen in the outside world and the attempts of individual oases in your mind to turn your attention to the information they are responsible for reminding you about. As discussed, these oases are keen to get your attention because the more time you spend mulling over those memories/issues/problems they are responsible for storing, the more electrical energy they're gifted, the stronger they become and the further up the hierarchy of your oases they rise. This is how we get obsessed with something. It's the result of an efficient oasis getting us to repeatedly dwell on a specific person, thing, or past event. Of course, you have many welcome and helpful oases, too. Like those that remind you that your favourite programme starts in an hour, to brush your teeth, or that today is a friend's birthday, so don't forget that birthday message.

Seventeen

A quick recap/overview of The Mind Theatre

The Mind Theatre is a circular space the size of a living room, with a swivel chair at its centre. The chair faces an all-encompassing, floor-to-ceiling, 180-degree screen that wraps around the front half of the Theatre and takes up the entirety of the view of the chair's occupant (you). **Exactly** as you're viewing the outside world right now. Behind the chair is a mirror image of what you're observing on the screen (seeing in the outside world).

Rising before the swivel chair, in easy reach, is the Lever of Focus. The Lever resembles a mechanism that switches train tracks from left to right and vice versa. **The Lever of Focus can only be locked in one of two positions**. It's either pulled to the right side, 2 0 clock position; this means the chair and your attention are facing the screen (your view of the outside world where you're living in the moment).

Alternatively, this Lever can be pulled to the left side, 10 0 clock position. This means the chair and your attention have turned 180 degrees and now face the back wall of your Theatre to focus **inwardly** on your thoughts.

The Lever of Focus is the key to acquiring your rightful control over your focus and ability to instruct your Green Factory to create endorphins.

Eighteen

The basics of how to take hold of your Lever of Focus and move it to the coveted right-side position

An unhelpful oasis may tell you that imagining your Mind Theatre with a convenient swivel chair and Lever of Focus before it is one thing, but how are you supposed to take hold of this all-important but *imaginary* Lever?

Well, nature is a clever beast. Genius, in fact. As such, it may be no coincidence that the five digits on a human hand match the number of senses we have: sight, sound, touch, smell, and taste. Your five senses are the four fingers and a thumb on your lever-pulling hand.

Here are some examples of how these individual digits/senses work:

The Smell Digit on your Lever-pulling hand

So, for instance, when you enter a coffee shop and smell coffee, the moment you notice and appreciate the smell, your Lever of Focus is pulled to the right-side position by this awareness and appreciation. The next moment, your Lever (and therefore your attention) will doubtless be pulled back to the left side by your thoughts. Still, for a wonderful second or two, you were savouring the smell of freshly roasted coffee using the right side of your mind.

Sound

Or, you might have walked into the coffee shop and heard a favourite song playing that pulled your Lever to the right side and took you out of your thoughts for a second or two as you hummed along. In this instance, your hearing (or the hearing digit on your Lever-pulling hand) has moved your Lever of Focus to the coveted right-side position.

Touch

If, when you opened the door to the coffee shop, you **noticed** that the handle felt grubby and sticky, your sense of touch (the touch digit on your Lever pulling hand) will have moved the Lever to the right side for a moment as you grimaced.

Taste

Or when you walked in, you were offered a free muffin sample, and you accepted. In this case, the delicious **taste** will move your Lever of Focus to the Right Side as you savour it.

Sight

And saving the best till last, you walk into the coffee shop to see the man or woman of your dreams. The sight digit on your Lever-pulling hand has wrapped itself around your Lever of Focus and moved it firmly to the right-side position as you look in wonder.

This is how each of your five senses can act as a finger on your Lever-pulling hand. Although, for instructing our Green Factory to create endorphins, we are predominately interested in sight, followed some distance behind by sound. Sight is more than powerful enough to pull this easily manoeuvred **magnetic** Lever to the right side.

Nineteen

Being in the moment

The first go at using sight to move and hold the Lever of Focus to the right-side position

The Right-Side Checklist

1. **Ensure that your gaze is ABOVE the central horizon**. Why? Because when your Lever moves to the left side position, and your chair swivels to face the back of your Mind Theatre, and you begin to dwell **inwardly** on your thoughts, your gaze invariably falls to the ground. When this happens, it's as though a shutter comes down to cover about two-thirds of your screen, making you unaware of what's happening around you. Think about when you've passed someone in the street with a lot on their mind; their gaze will be towards the ground and, while absorbed in the file of an oasis, they don't even notice you. This

is why keeping your gaze **above your screen's central horizon** assists in holding your Lever of Focus to the right-side using sight. It also sends a loud and clear message to any oases trying to get your attention and draw your Lever back to the left side: "Far from there being a threat that requires stressing over, something welcome and fascinating's going on, so let me enjoy it!"

2. As you gaze **above** the central horizon, open your eyes a little wider as you would if you turned a corner and saw something extraordinary.

3. Finally, while engaging in the above, we'd like you to raise the corners of your closed mouth into a smile. Why? As we know, the muscles you use when smiling communicate to your oases that all is well in your world; therefore, returning to their file to overthink a problem, let alone the assistance of your fight or flight response, is not required.

Let's have a go now. Please combine the above three points. **However, don't focus your sight on**

one thing or a specific place. Your goal is to focus on and allow the **entirety** of the extraordinary Imax-pressed-up-against-your-face-like vista that fills your vision to flow like a river of colours and textures into your Mind Theatre to be mirrored on its back screen, thereby washing away and **keeping your thoughts that are trying to get your attention quiet.** Remember, the Lever of Focus can only be locked into the right or left-side positions. If **anything** occurs to you (springs to mind) while attempting to hold your Lever of Focus to the right-side using sight, it means that your **Lever and your focus** have swung back to the left-side to register and consider these thoughts.

With this first attempt, your goal is to hold your Lever of Focus to the right-side for 5+ seconds without **any interruptions from your oases/thoughts.** When done successfully, you'll be washing away/keeping your thoughts quiet with the **tsunami of vision** you're focusing on/welcoming through your screen to be mirrored (or **captured** like an old-fashioned box camera would capture an image on a slate) on the back of your Mind Theatre. Just like those times when you're watching something so **enjoyable and engrossing**, it successfully holds your attention and blissfully keeps your thoughts quiet. **During these happy times, you are naturally telling your Green Factory that it's time to work on those endorphins that make you want to seek out this positive experience again.** Like everything worthwhile in life, practice makes perfect. If you can perfect this level of right-sided focus in response to pangs of anxiety or dread, even for just a few seconds, it will empower you to positively affect your state of mind and health in life-changing ways. We call this 5+ seconds of right-sided focus going into **Thrust.** Just as a jet engine draws air into it to propel the plane forward, you are consciously focusing on and allowing a tsunami of vision to flood into your Mind Theatre to **shut your thoughts out** and propel yourself forward into a positive and mindful place where you're present and **living in the moment** for 5+ seconds. The opposite of Thrust is Contraction when you're deep in repetitive and stressful thoughts. Which is where you would have ended up had you not gone into Thrust.

Twenty

The Mind Theatre Curtains

To help make your new positive message to your Green Factory as robust as possible, it can be helpful to imagine that a circular curtain is wrapped around the inside of your Mind Theatre. Now, focusing **above** the central horizon, imagine a hairline crack running down the centre of the curtains, where they meet directly in front of you on your screen. Next, concentrate and **imagine** drawing back both the left and right sides of the curtains as though you're revealing and **revelling in** the view of the outside world behind them for the first time. Imagine gradually pulling the curtains back around yourself/your Mind Theatre so that the image can flood onto its back screen, where it **keeps your thoughts quiet** for 5+ seconds.

As you imagine peeling back both sections of the curtain from the centre of the screen and **successfully shut out thoughts**, you may experience what we can only describe as an auto smile. It's as though the mechanism (your concentration) pulling the imagined circular curtain asunder is attached to the smile muscles in your face, automatically lifting them from the corners of your **closed mouth** into a smile. In the same way as you smile automatically when you see/encounter something genuinely uplifting or awe-inspiring.

When you achieve this level of vision-welcoming focus, it's akin to firing a broadside of cannons and blasting your mind with a positive message that says, "This is great! So, get to work, Green Factory!"

Twenty-one

The Two Pen Pully System

The Two Pen Pully System will assist in drawing back the curtains and going into Thrust. Unsurprisingly, you will need two pens (or two pencils).

Hold the pens at arm's length. Press them together, side by side, with their nibs facing the ceiling. Now focus on the pens and **slowly** bring them closer to your face. When the pens are just a few inches from your face, and you start to lose focus/feel yourself going boss-eyed, **observe and concentrate** on the feeling of eye and forehead strain as you struggle to maintain your focus and not go boss-eyed. Now, having brought the pens close enough to your face to have to struggle against going boss-eyed, pull them **slowly** apart and around to your ears as though **revealing** the view behind them and, as you do, bring the edges of your **closed mouth** up into a smile as you welcome the tsunami of vision into your Mind Theatre to be captured on the back wall and go into Thrust for 5 + seconds. During these 5+ seconds, attempt to maintain the **same determination** you felt when struggling to keep your eyes focused when the pens reached a close enough position to your face for you to start to go boss-eyed. If your concentration and focus are dedicated enough, you may experience a slight juddering in your neck that causes your head to judder. **If this occurs, it's to be welcomed**. This mental determination required to keep the pens in focus should be practised and explored.

Of course, the two pens represent the edges of the curtains you're pulling back around yourself. The sensation of pressure/discomfort as you struggle to focus on the pens and **not** go boss-eyed is important because it makes tangible a higher level of concentration required while holding the Lever to the right-side in Thrust.

More about the neck juddering sensation you may experience

When the tsunami of vision is captured on the back screen of your Mind Theatre and **successfully** keeps your thoughts quiet, the muscles in your neck might judder (like an ornament on a shelf at the onset of a slight tremor caused by an earthquake). This slight friction/juddering occurs due to a magnetic tug of war between your determination to keep the Lever to the right-side using the tsunami of vision and the determination of an oasis to pull it back to the left-side and get you dwelling on the information inside its file. The more you pay attention to and observe this friction, the more authority you'll gain over your Lever of Focus. Not everyone will experience this juddering effect. Don't be concerned if you don't. And it might happen at some point in the future when you least expect it.

Twenty-two

The Eyes Closed Technique

Initially, you may find it easier to imagine this parting in the centre of the curtains with your eyes closed. With your eyes closed, as you draw the now imagined pens aside from the centre of your darkened screen, imagine the darkness wrapping around the entirety of your Mind Theatre.

Whereas holding the Lever of Focus to the right-side with eyes open may trigger an auto smile and a slight juddering in your neck muscles as the images flood into your Mind Theatre and successfully keep your thoughts quiet, when done with your eyes closed, the judder in your neck may be taken to another level of intensity. It's as though particles of tiredness clogging up your mind are being shaken loose to evaporate, leaving you feeling re-energised when you open your eyes and continue your day. Again, this **valuable and welcome friction** is caused by your determination to hold your Lever to the right-side and go into Thrust using the tsunami of darkness that's flooding into your Mind Theatre and the attempts of your oases to get you to abandon Thrust and go into Contraction by entering their files and mulling over the information they contain.

Twenty-three

The importance of breathing normally while in Thrust

While holding the Lever to the right-side in Thrust, your breathing should be relaxed, normal, and through your nose. Never consciously take deeper breaths while holding your Lever to the right-side. It's likely that when you are doing so successfully, you may naturally feel the need to breathe a little more deeply like you would if you turned a corner and witnessed something intoxicating.

<u>The folly of deep breathing</u>

As we discussed earlier, taking deep breaths is something we do when we're under threat and gives the Red Factory a green light. Intuitive midwives were the only branch of medicine that long ago realised the importance of not deliberately taking deeper breaths during times of stress. Therefore, they tell women in labour to place the emphasis of their breathing on their exhale by blowing out in short, sharp bursts. This helps to calm the woman giving birth. Each little exhale or puff is like a tiny message that communicates the message, "I'm fine, overprotective oases! I don't need any more cortisol, thanks!" Advising women in labour to take deep breaths would communicate the opposite, that assistance is required from fight or flight, and they'd quickly find themselves in a state of breathless panic. The worst advice you can give someone when they're anxious is to take deep breaths. Yet people do it all the time because they've heard others share the same advice.

So, to complete our Lever-pulling to the right training, we will borrow something from those clever midwives. As you draw the physical or imagined pens aside, we'd like you to exhale through your nose as though you have just spotted something that's **literally breathtaking**.

Twenty-four

The Five Steps

For successfully holding your Lever to the right-side and prompting your Green Factory to manufacture endorphins that replace heady feelings of dread

1. Make sure your gaze is **up** above the central horizon (because whenever you engage with your thoughts, your gaze drops towards the ground).

2. Exhale/sigh contentedly through your nose as you pull the **physical or imagined pens** apart from the centre of your screen as though you've just happened upon something literally breathtaking.

3. As you do so, raise the edges of your closed mouth into a smile, and then breathe normally through your nose if possible.

4. As you draw the pens **slowly** apart and around to the sides of your head, focus on and welcome the extraordinary vista of colours and textures that take up the **entirety** of your vision into your Mind Theatre to be mirrored on its back wall and, in so doing, keep your Lever of Focus held to the **right-side** and **shut out** your thoughts for 5+ seconds.

5. During these 5+ seconds, your oases will attempt to distract you and pull your Lever back to the left-side. Prevent this by doubling down, opening your eyes a little wider, and revelling in the view through your **all-encompassing Imax pressed against your face screen**. During this process, expect a tug-of-war between your efforts to hold your Lever to the right-side and shut out your thoughts and attempts of your oases to pull it to the left-side and get you thinking inside their files. As a result of this tug of war, you may experience slight juddering in your neck, which

shakes your head a little. If this happens, it's to be welcomed. It can indicate that you've hit the sweet spot concentration-wise. The greater the juddering, the more you're winning the tug of war, going into Thrust and successfully allowing the visual tsunami before you to flood into your Mind Theatre to keep your thoughts quiet **and** communicate to your Green Factory that you're viewing something breathtaking that endorphins must accompany to make you seek out this positive experience again.

Twenty-five

The Positive Reset

Taking stock of how you feel

Having successfully held your Lever to the right-side for 5+ seconds, it will be time to take stock of how you feel. As we know, the dark cloud of dread that descends on our mind is the result of cortisol made by the Red Factory. However, holding the Lever to the right-side for 5+ seconds and going into Thrust has the opposite effect. In Thrust, we're mimicking gazing upon something awe-inspiring, which prompts the Green Factory to create endorphins that complement the experience. These endorphins replace the cortisol and blast away the dark cloud, leaving us feeling better.

At most, several **successful** Lever holding to the right-side actions in succession will trigger the production of sufficient endorphins to restore peace of mind. Therefore, being aware and taking stock of how you feel in the seconds that follow a right-side hold is important. It lets you gauge whether an overprotective oasis got the message loudly enough. Or whether you must redouble your efforts and fire another broadside of positivity. Remember, you have an **endless supply** of positive endorphins at your Lever-to-the-right/going into Thrust holding fingertips.

The first time you experience this Positive Reset, this blasting away of a dark cloud of anxiety or dread to reclaim peace of mind with the assistance of your Green Factory and knowing you can do it **whenever** necessary, it is nothing short of a life-changing moment.

A timely reminder about baulking

A new **Baulking Oases** will attempt to stop you from learning these new skills and, if successful, raise its status amongst your hierarchy of oases. Your new Balking Oases will ask you questions in your own voice, such as, "Can you *really* do this?" "Isn't this nonsense?" "Is this really for you?" and a dozen others as it attempts to get you to abandon what you're doing and return to your files to overthink/stress over their contents. At such times, respond by taking hold of your Lever and holding it **firmly** to the right side, flushing this unhelpful Balking Oases away with a tsunami of vision.

Final thoughts on the Lever of Focus

As well as a tool to chart a new course away from stress, anxiety or depression, the Lever places you in a wonderful, positive, and healthy state of mind **whenever** you pull it to the right-side. One where you're aware of your surroundings and **living in the moment.** At such times, your mind is open and responsive to inspiration, intuition, and ingenuity. These three are possible when the Lever is held to the right; you're in Thrust, and the outside is rushing into your mind. The opposite of this, the Lever, being on the left and being deep in thought, is akin to your mind being in Contraction and closed to the outside. This is why prolonged thinking is exhausting and stressful. And why all those things we seek for relaxation and enjoyment, like watching sports or films, listening to music or reading books, etc., **require us to hold the Lever to the right** to focus on and enjoy them. Moving forward, be aware that you don't need a great film or book to be fully aware and live in the moment. It has the same effect when you're genuinely *seeing* what's before your eyes, so it's mirrored on the back wall of your Mind Theatre.

Pulling out the weeds and cultivating the flowers or The Oases Flush

We are all aware when an oasis with a distressing topic/memory arrives in our thoughts. If we begin to overthink this topic/issue, it makes us more stressed. The bait the oasis uses is the possibility of finding a solution at the bottom of its file. Remember, the answers are **never** found re-treading old ground in these files. The solution will come when you least expect it, when you're relaxing, and your Lever is pulled to the right-side naturally. This is when inspiration and intuition are possible.

The moment you find yourself gazing into the well-trodden abyss of the information in the file of an oasis, go into Thrust and flush the oasis away for a few seconds. If you react this way quickly, the effort to flush away the reminder of the issue is minimal. A few seconds of right-sided focus will do the trick. However, if you delve into its file, the further you venture/dwell on its stress-inflaming contents, the more cortisol will be created by your Red Factory. This means more effort with your Lever and assistance from your Green Factory will be required to achieve a positive reset. So be vigilant for these unwelcome oases. Like a farmer sitting on a porch with a shotgun in case a fox should threaten his chickens. Initially, you will be coaxed back into overthinking in these stressful files. The key is the **speed** at which you notice that you've ventured into a stressful minefield and then grab your Lever to leave it and flush the oasis away with a tsunami of positive vision for a few seconds that will bring your Green Factory to your aid. With practice, your awareness of these troublesome oases will grow, and you will react more quickly.

In conclusion

For some, the PDA **physical** message detailed in the first half of this book will be their way to get their Green Factory firing on all cylinders on their behalf. For others, it will be the mental message of going into Thrust. Once both are mastered, they can be combined to extraordinary effect. This is demonstrated in Charlie's Potential Morning from Hell.

Twenty-six

Charlie's Potential Morning from Hell

Examples of how to use the stressbusting techniques you've learned

Charlie's boss, Avery Jones, has chosen him to give an important presentation at 9 a.m. Charlie left home early but not having access to a crystal ball, failed to foresee the emergency road works that have slowed his motoring progress to a stop/start crawl. Charlie grabs his phone to call and apologise to Avery and takes a deep breath as he realises the battery's flat as he forgot to charge it last night. Charlie's Avery Oasis is lightning quick to take advantage of the situation and sends an image of the disappointment on Avery's face when Charlie doesn't turn up on time and hasn't even bothered to call to explain to his conscious screen. Charlie's Avery Oasis used this image of Avery to ask Charlie: 'Is letting Avery down a threat?` It's a question accompanied by some butterflies in

Charlie's stomach hastily manufactured by his Red Factory, now working with Charlie's Avery Oasis. Both are chomping at the prospect of being "useful" to Charlie in the face of this apparent threat. Charlie's Avery Oasis at the chance of getting him to overthink the potential pitfalls and negative consequences of being late for the presentation and disappointing Avery, and the Red Factory of being useful in making Charlie hyper-alert to this threat by manufacturing cortisol in the mistaken belief that Avery is a sabre tooth tiger, and with these two on the case, Avery might as well be a sabre tooth tiger as Charlie gazes through the rear bumper of the stationary car in front into the file of his Avery Oasis and licks his dry lips.

A new and valuable oasis to the rescue!

Earlier that week, Charlie read a book called Stressbusting For the 20th Century. As a result, another oasis in his mind, his recently created Green Factory Oasis, manages to elbow its way onto his conscious screen and remind him that the precipice of stress and anxiety he's teetering on is entirely due to him passively **allowing** his Red Factory to do this to him even though it will serve no useful purpose. The cortisol it's producing might have been useful if Charlie needed to scamper up a tree to escape the jaws of a lion, but trees and big cats are conspicuous by their absence inside his car. What's more, when he does eventually arrive at work in the cortisol-addled, immune system-pummelled state he'll be in if he allows this to continue, he'll be little use to himself or anyone so... Charlie looks up from the car's bumper in front, and the words 'My Green Factory` quiver on his dry lips. Desperate to put in a request for some immune system-boosting endorphins to counteract and replace the cortisol, Charlie attempts to exhale forcibly but somehow manages to draw a deep breath instead, which draws more butterflies into his stomach, having inadvertently instructed his Red Factory to manufacture extra for him. And when Charlie does manage an exhale, it's more of a gasp accompanied by a whimper. But Charlie's Green Factory oasis, keen to make its way up his hierarchy of oases by influencing him, shoulders a baulking oasis that's just told Charlie,' You'll never be able to do this!` out of the way and reminds Charlie that he wanted an opportunity to try this new technique he's been practising at home while in a genuinely stressful situation. 'Isn't this the ideal opportunity? And what have you got to lose?' Charlie nods and, ignoring his **every impulse to breathe more deeply**, he instead, and **for the first time in his life when facing a stressful situation**, **exhales forcibly** as though he's blowing up a balloon with a single, sustained, powerful exhale that lasts 5 seconds. At the same time, his hand goes to his abs, and reassuringly, he feels them tighten. Charlie's Green Factory Oasis reminds him to close his mouth as this will ensure that he breaths through his nostrils, which, thankfully, are much smaller than his mouth and will limit the air that can carry butterflies back into his stomach. So, there he is, holding his tightened abs in place, having expelled **all the air** from his lungs as though mid hysterical laugh when his Green Factory Oasis reminds him to 'Smile! No, keep your mouth closed, remember?' Charlie has entered his Green Factory Operational Zone. It is an immensely positive place that perfectly reproduces what he does when laughing hysterically. And he's done this despite having been teetering on the edge of free-fall just moments before. It's an immensely positive action as far as his mind/body system is concerned and one he would never have taken, not in a million years, had he not read about the possibility of doing so earlier in the week. Indeed, it has taken humanity a million years to be self-aware enough to take control of their responses in this way in times of mounting stress and anxiety. Two, three, four, five seconds pass, and Charlie exits the Green Factory Operational Zone by relaxing his abs and breathing normally into his stomach again. 'It's time to take stock of how you feel,' his Green Factory Oasis reminds him. As Charlie gazes at the stationery cars around him with a faraway expression, it occurs to him that the butterflies of stress and anxiety that were intent on having a rave in his stomach seconds before have been well and truly crushed by his abs and expelled by his no-nonsense exhale. He undoubtedly feels better for his actions from the neck down, thanks to this and the presence of the endorphins his Green Factory would have manufactured since he successfully entered his Green Factory Operational Zone.

But the dark cloud of dread he also felt in his head, resulting from his Red Factory switching on the cortisol sprinklers between his ears, is still somewhat present. Charlie's new Thrust Oasis, buoyed by the success of the Green Factory Oasis, sends a reminder to his conscious screen that 'Holding your Lever of Focus to the right-side and going into Thrust for just a few seconds will blast away this dark cloud of dread by instructing your Green Factory to make endorphins to replace the cortisol that's still lingering in your mind.` Desperate to do something about this heady feeling of dread, Charlie ignores an attempt by his Avery Oasis to get him into its file by suggesting he thinks about the negative things his work colleagues will soon be saying about him. Instead, and for the first time in his life at such a moment, he deliberately switches his attention away from such a pressing file to his surroundings through his all-encompassing, Imax-like screen. 'Concentrate hard so that everything on your screen/seeing floods into your Mind Theatre so that it's mirrored on its back wall, flushing away the Avery oasis,` his Thrust oasis reminds him before it too is flushed away when Charlie goes into Thrust by pulling his Lever of Focus to the right-side by successfully focusing on the **all-encompassing view** and exhaling contentedly as he does so. Because Charlie is sending his Green Factory a message **directly** from his Mind Theatre instead of from his diaphragm and ads, he's firing up/ensuring endorphins are released in his brain where the dark cloud of dread/cortisol remains. Charlie's Green Factory releases endorphins in this way **whenever** Charlie is apparently filled with awe by something breathtaking that's happening right in front of him. He has even experienced a wonderful tingling sensation in his head on these rare past occasions, thanks to the endorphins.

Back to the present. Charlie would never pay something this much **going into Thrust attention** if what he beheld wasn't extraordinary/breathtaking. Unable to see through his eyes, Charlie's Green Factory has no idea that he's now apparently mesmerised by a group of stationary cars with frustrated occupants below an overcast sky. For a split second, Charlie sees an image of a now angry-looking Avery checking his watch. Charlie knows this means his Avery Oasis had successfully pulled his Lever back to the left side 10 o'clock position. He could never have seen this image otherwise. A tug-of-war between Charlie and his Avery oasis is underway. Charlie grabs his Lever of Focus by re-focusing his attention on the **entirety** of the view through his screen, successfully flushing away and silencing his Avery Oasis and even takes advantage of someone's sustained honk on a car horn to use the hearing digit of his Lever holding hand to assist his vision digit. Extraordinarily, given the circumstances, Charlie finds himself **fully present in the moment**, a rare place to be and would typically require watching something genuinely entertaining and engrossing to keep his thoughts this quiet. He realises he's smiling from the corners of his closed mouth, just as he might be if watching a hoped-for conclusion to a favourite movie. And is this slight juddering in his neck that moves his head a fraction from side to side as he successfully goes into Thrust a natural by-product of the tug of war between him and his Avery oasis or is he consciously doing it because he'd read how it might happen when in Thrust. Charlie doesn't know or care, as this feels much better than the stress-fuelled, overthinking alternative his Avery Oasis had in store for him.

The moment Charlie takes his hand off the Lever of Focus and leaves Thrust, his Thrust oasis, now stronger and higher up his hierarchy of oases for proving useful, reminds Charlie that it's time for him to take stock of how he feels. Due to his Green Factory's great work releasing endorphins in his brain during the 5 seconds that he **successfully** held his Lever to the right-side in Thrust, the dark cloud of negativity and dread has pretty much been dissipated, which means he's able to see things from a clearer, more realistic and positive perspective. I.e., the road works were not his fault; nobody died, phones run out of juice, and this could have happened to anyone. Avery and his colleagues will see the funny side, and it's absolutely **not** the end of the world.

Charlie might have needed to go into Thrust again for another 5+ seconds to blast away his heady feeling of dread and achieve this clear-thinking perspective. Something he could easily have done had he taken stock of how he felt, and the cloud of dread hadn't been lifted sufficiently. He has access to limitless immune system-boosting endorphins at his Lever to the right-side and going into Thrust fingertips.

Charlie's journey to work was an example of how the physical FDA Method and the mental technique of going in Thrust can be used in a stressful situation. Charlie's journey to work was like a rollercoaster ride. One in which he started in the seat of someone whose immune system was about to be pummelled by cortisol but, through his positive actions, was able to move into the seat of someone who responded to the ride in a way that instructed his Green Factory to take over. The same principle can be applied to any situation.

Charlie arrives at work in a significantly better place thanks to enlisting the help of his Green

Factory than he would have otherwise, and he's not nearly as late as his Avery Oasis had told him he would be when he first hit the roadworks. With a memory stick with his presentation in hand, he goes into the photocopier room to print it out to discover maintenance working on it due to a malfunction. They tell him they should have it in working within a few minutes, so he takes a seat and isn't surprised when his Avery Oasis tries its luck by using its remaining energy (having been denied the feed it had hoped for in the car) to ask Charlie 'After all that is this broken printer going to ruin everything? Isn't that your rotten luck?` Again, Charlie finds himself gazing into the stressful abyss of the file of his Avery Oasis. Thanks to Charlie's good work in the car, his energy levels remain high, the opposite of his Avery Oasis, and with the flutter of a tiny butterfly in his stomach, he decides to enter the Lesser Golf Ball Sized Zone and expels it with a quick half second exhale. He holds his **slightly** tightened abs in place by breathing through his nose into his upper chest and raising his mouth's corners into a smile. If someone were to look at Charlie, they'd see someone who looked calm and appeared to have something faintly amusing on their mind. While in the Lesser Golf Ball Sized Zone, Charlie's abs aren't mid hysterical laugh as they would if he'd blown up a full-size imaginary balloon to enter the full-on Green Factory Operational Zone. In the Lesser Golf Ball Sized Zone, his abs are held as though he's chuckling at something faintly amusing for an extended period, which instructs his Green Factory to manufacture immune system-boosting endorphins subtlety to match the experience he's apparently having. And the expulsion of the small butterfly when entering the Zone instantly relieved the anxiety in his gut.

Charlie's Avery Oasis is still hanging around like a bad smell. Aware that his Lever of Focus is the best way of dealing with it, Charlie gently takes hold of his Lever by **simply switching the focus of his attention to the view through his screen** so that it enters his Mind Theatre to be captured on its back wall. Charlie discovers that, in a less stressful situation such as this, when his energy levels are good, this more relaxed version of Thrust (**simply making sure he's consciously aware of his surroundings through his screen**) is enough to flush the weakened Avery Oasis away, stay out of its file and remain present in the moment.

Seeing the woods for the trees

The comforting fact is that by **consciously switching our attention** to the view through our screen and going into a more relaxed version of Thrust, the benefits are not unlike exhaling and holding our abs gently in the Lesser Golf Ball Sized Zone. It's a means of instructing the Green Factory to create low levels of endorphins using vision to place us in the moment (something we would normally only do when watching/experiencing something enjoyable). So, Charlie has avoided being in Contraction in his thoughts, stressing over the time it's taking to fix the printer. A hundred-meter sprinter would describe this conscious switch of focus, this visual awareness, as being in the Zone as they shut out doubts and distractions by focusing on the finishing line.

A minute later, presentation document in hand and due in the boardroom, Charlie hurries to the elevator and squeezes through its closing doors in the nick of time. He steps behind the only other elevator occupant and wills it to start its journey to the fifth floor. The seconds pass, but alas for Charlie, who hasn't felt comfortable in elevators since he had a panic attack in a stuck one some years before, the elevator lurches up before coming to a grinding halt. On the previous occasion, he hyperventilated while the other passengers did their best to reassure and calm him. Charlie's Red Factory went above and beyond that day and busted a gut to give him that panic attack. Today, Charlie remembers what he read about his body needing a massive amount of extra oxygen to make a panic attack happen. He finds an ironic smile when he remembers how he had gasped for air like it was going out of fashion on the previous occasion.

Back to the present, the other passenger in the elevator looks at him, shrugs and says this happens sometimes, but maintenance will be on it right away. As she pushes a button and calls for assistance, behind her, Charlie wastes no time in expelling the gathering butterflies in his gut by blowing up an enormous imaginary balloon with a single sustained exhale and, having expelled the butterfly-addled air from his lungs, holds his tightened abs firmly in place by breathing through his nose into his upper chest and does his best to smile. Charlie has entered his Green Factory Operational Zone. This doesn't only deny his Red Factory the extra oxygen it must have to pull off a panic attack; it means that his mind/body system will have to focus on managing and distributing the available oxygen to his organs. What's more, this decisive action has taken him out of the seat of the panic-stricken rider of the rollercoaster and placed him into the seat of someone who's embracing it and does not consider it a threat—a call to his Green Factory to take over from the Red. For good measure, Charlie switches attention away from his Elevator Panic Oasis, which is basically asking, 'Are you certain there isn't a lion inside this elevator like the last time?` by going into Thrust. Such is Charlie's determination to flush away and reassure his Elevator Panic Oasis that no lion is present; his neck muscles judder a little, moving his head from side to side for several seconds as the view inside the elevator floods into his Mind Theatre. The other passenger turns to look at him, and he takes his hand off his Lever, relaxes his abs, and realises, much to his mental and physical relief, that all things considered, he feels okay. Indeed, the threat of the panic attack seems to have passed, and he's ready to enter his Green Factory Operational Zone again should his Red Factory have another go. And the comfort of knowing this goes a long way to helping him take things in his stride.

Charlie makes it to the presentation room fifteen minutes later, where Avery and his colleagues commiserate with him about his Elevator experience, and his presentation goes well. How different Avery's morning would have been had it been spent reacting in a way that meant his Red Factory had his back and not his Green Factory.

Conclusion

The accumulative effects of directing our Green Factory to assist us over weeks, months and years are immeasurable. Replacing cortisol with endorphins in this way could potentially add years of healthy life. Not to mention having fought off any number of illnesses due to our immune system being more robust.

This book is concise for a reason. We've stuck to the salient points and humbly advise you to read through it several times and jot down things that resonate most.

Again, we encourage you to master both the mental response of going into Thrust by switching your Lever of Focus to the right-side and the physical F.D.A. Method by mastering your positive message muscles. With both in your arsenal, you'll naturally gravitate towards one or the other (or both), depending on the situation.

A review or rating on Amazon would be much appreciated as it will assist others in finding this book. The human mind is endlessly fascinating and revealing, so any observations or discoveries of your own having applied the techniques taught in this book would be greatly welcomed in the reviews. They might also help others.

If you have any questions about the F.D.A. Method or Thrust, you are very welcome to email us at stress.b.workshop@gmail.com

And finally, we wish you all the best at becoming the foreman of your Green Factory and embracing life's rollercoaster ride!

Immediate goals sheet

Name the most dominant oasis/tripwire oasis in your mind (for instance, for Charlie in part one of this book, it would be his Mole Oasis)

....

List 3 questions it has used as bait to tempt you back into its file to stress over a perceived problem.

1.................................

2.................................

3.................................

Name a baited question in the form of an image it has placed on your screen to tempt you back in (for Charlie, it was the less-than-reassuring expression on the face of his doctor) ....

Awareness is the first step. Your fightback against stress with the aid of your Green Factory begins here.

Made in the USA
Monee, IL
26 September 2023

43477866R00066